The Effortless Bread Machine Cookbook

Bake Perfect Homemade White, Whole Grain, Sweet, and Gluten-Free Loaves with Foolproof Tips and Real Ingredients

Abigail Douglas

Table of Contents

Disclaimer

The information, recipes, and suggestions provided in The Effortless Bread Machine Cookbook are intended for general informational and educational purposes only. While every effort has been made to ensure accuracy and clarity, the author and publisher make no guarantees regarding results, as outcomes may vary based on the brand and model of bread machine used, ingredient quality, altitude, climate, and individual kitchen practices.

This cookbook is not a substitute for professional dietary advice, medical guidance, or allergen management. If you have food allergies, dietary restrictions, or health conditions, please consult with a qualified healthcare provider or nutritionist before trying any new recipe.

All recipes are developed with standard home kitchen equipment and widely available ingredients. Always read and follow the safety instructions provided by your bread machine manufacturer before operating your appliance.

The author and publisher disclaim any liability, loss, or risk incurred as a consequence—direct or indirect—of the use and application of any of the content in this book.

All product names, brands, or references to appliances are used for descriptive purposes only and are not affiliated with or endorsed by this publication.

Preface

There's a quiet kind of magic in baking bread at home.

Not the complicated kind that takes hours of kneading or leaves your kitchen looking like a science lab—but the kind that fills the air with warmth, the kind that turns simple ingredients into something meaningful. The kind that's… effortless.

This book was born from that desire—for ease, for flavor, and for something real.

Whether you're brand new to baking or someone rediscovering the joy of homemade bread, **The Effortless Bread Machine Cookbook** is your go-to guide for making soft white loaves, hearty whole grain bread, indulgent sweet treats, and even gluten-free staples right in your own kitchen—with minimal fuss and maximum satisfaction.

Inside these pages, you'll find:

- Easy bread machine recipes for beginners that take the guesswork out of baking

- Homemade white, whole grain, sweet, and gluten-free bread recipes that deliver comfort and variety

- Foolproof tips to prevent common problems like collapsed loaves or dense textures

- Savory breads, sweet loaves, dinner rolls, sandwich buns, pizza dough, cinnamon swirls, and more

- Fun, hands-on projects for kids like PB&J swirl bread, rainbow loaves, and mini bread animals

- Smart ways to transform leftover bread into croutons, French toast, bread pudding, and beyond

But more than just recipes, this is a kitchen companion. One that helps you build confidence in using your bread machine, explore the joy of creating something with your hands, and share nourishing, delicious results with the people you love.

Every recipe in this book has been thoughtfully developed to be doable, dependable, and deeply satisfying—whether you're craving **a classic white sandwich loaf**, a **soft dinner roll**, or a **gluten-free multigrain bread** that doesn't crumble when sliced.

And if you've ever asked, *"Why did my bread collapse?"* or "How do I get that bakery-style crust?"—you'll find clear, practical answers in the **Troubleshooting & Pro Tips** chapter, designed to support you every step of the way.

I believe anyone can bake amazing bread with the right guidance—and a machine that does most of the work for you. You don't need to be an expert. You don't need a long list of ingredients. You just need the desire to try.

So dust off that bread machine. Flip to any page. And let's make something warm, something simple, and something that fills more than just your kitchen.

Welcome to the effortless side of baking.

Let's get started.

Introduction

Why Bread, Why Now?

There's something ancient and sacred about the act of baking bread. The soft resistance of dough between your fingers. The warm, yeasty aroma that fills the house. The golden crust cracking as a knife slices through, revealing a steaming, tender interior. Bread is more than food—it's memory. It's comfort. It's tradition passed through the hands of grandmothers, shared across dinner tables, and now reshaped for modern life by a quiet little hero on your kitchen counter: the bread machine.

For years, bread machines were dismissed as outdated or clunky, pushed to the back of cabinets or sold off at garage sales. But today, they're staging a quiet comeback and for good reason.

We're in a season of life where people want more control over what they eat. Rising food costs, questionable store-bought ingredients, and a yearning for real, nourishing meals have reignited the love for homemade bread. But unlike traditional baking, which can be time-consuming and intimidating, the bread machine offers a shortcut to simplicity without sacrificing quality, flavor, or that soul-satisfying magic.

Why the Bread Machine is Back

You don't need to be a trained baker to make incredible bread. You don't even need to measure with laboratory precision. What you do need is a willingness to try, and a tool that does the hard part for you.

Bread machines are no longer bulky appliances collecting dust—they're smart, sleek, and perfect for:

Busy families who want fresh bread with dinner but don't

have time to knead and rise.

- **Seniors** looking for gentle, homemade recipes without preservatives or excess sodium.

- **Health-conscious eaters** who want control over their ingredients (think: gluten-free, whole grain, low-sugar).

- **Anyone on a budget**, because let's face it: baking bread at home is drastically cheaper than that $6 artisan loaf at the market.

And when you're using just a few whole ingredients—flour, water, yeast, maybe a touch of honey or olive oil—you're not just feeding your body, you're **nourishing your home**.

Store-Bought vs. Homemade: There Is a Difference

We've all seen the ingredient lists on packaged bread—unpronounceable additives, preservatives, and sugars in five different disguises. Even "healthy" loaves can be misleading.

Homemade bread, on the other hand, is honest. You know every single ingredient going into it. You can keep it simple or make it bold. You can adjust the texture, the sweetness, the saltiness. You can bake with purpose—dietary, emotional, or seasonal.

And maybe most importantly, **you can taste the difference**. Store-bought bread is fine until you've had real, fresh, warm bread from your own kitchen. Then… there's no going back.

What You'll Need to Get Started

No fancy tricks. No long grocery lists. Just a few tools and ingredients, and you're ready to make bread that rivals any bakery.

The Machine

You'll want **a reliable bread machine**—nothing too complex. Most recipes in this book were tested on standard 1.5–2 lb capacity machines with basic functions like:

- Basic/White
- Whole Wheat
- Dough Only
- Sweet
- Rapid Bake

Brands like Zojirushi, Hamilton Beach, Cuisinart, or Panasonic will work just fine—this book isn't brand-dependent.

Measuring Tools

Accuracy matters in baking, especially with flour and

yeast. Keep these on hand:

- Measuring cups & spoons
- A digital kitchen scale (optional but helpful)
- A small rubber spatula or wooden spoon

Core Ingredients to Stock

You don't need a bakery's pantry. Just these essentials will take you far:

- **Bread flour or all-purpose flour**
- **Active dry yeast or instant yeast**
- **Salt** (fine sea salt works well)
- **Sweetener:** honey, sugar, or maple syrup
- **Liquid:** filtered water, milk, or plant-based alternatives
- **Oil or butter**, depending on the recipe

Optional: herbs, nuts, seeds, dried fruits, cheeses, oats, whole wheat flour, gluten-free blends—many of these will be introduced in later chapters.

The Promise of This Book

This is not a book filled with complicated recipes or long ingredient lists. It's a real-life kitchen companion designed for people who want **fast, reliable, delicious bread** with little effort. Each recipe was tested for simplicity, flavor, and flexibility. Whether you're a brand-new baker or someone rediscovering the joy of homemade bread, you'll find recipes here that work.

You'll also find something less tangible, but just as essential—**confidence**. Every successful loaf builds trust in yourself. Trust that yes, you can bake. You can create. You can make something nourishing from just five ingredients and a machine.

Welcome to a kitchen experience that's wholesome, joyful, and just the right amount of nostalgic. Let's bake some magic.

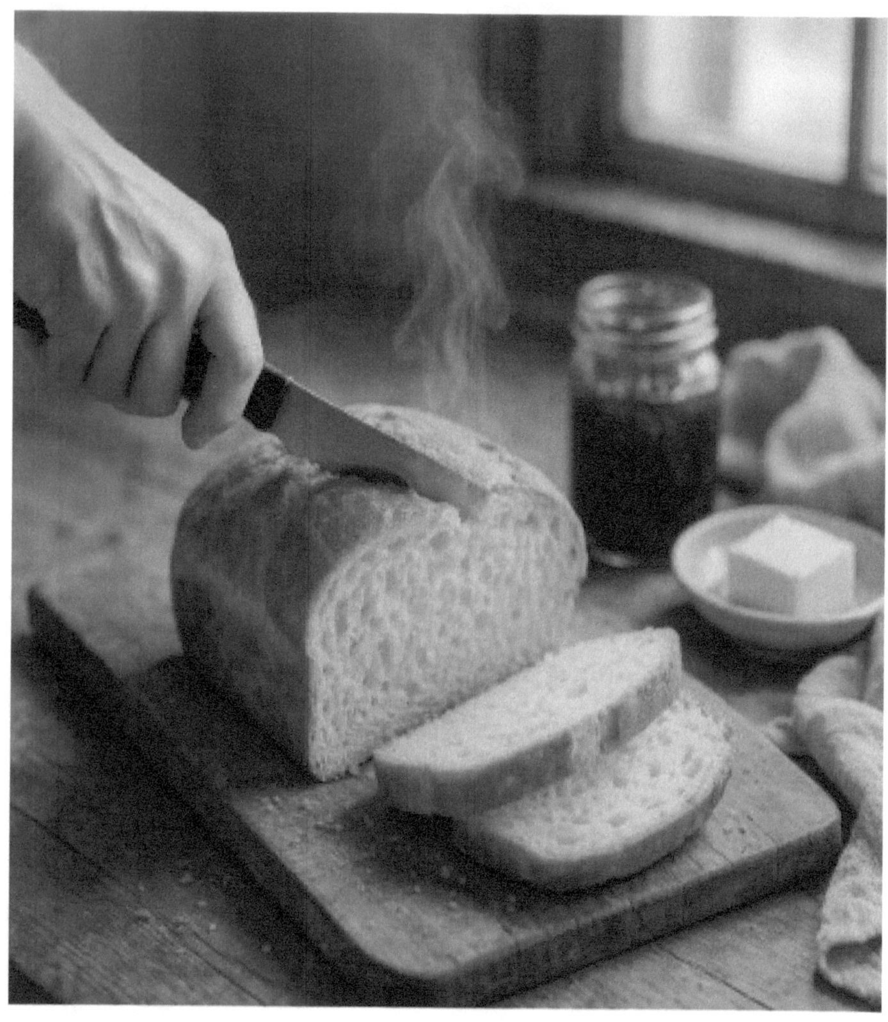

Chapter 1

Bread Machine Basics Made Simple

There's a kind of quiet magic to waking up to the scent of freshly baked bread especially when all you did was press a button the night before. But before we get to the loaves that will warm your kitchen and fill your soul, let's slow down for a moment and get to know the machine behind the magic.

A bread machine might look like a mysterious box at first, full of buttons, cycles, and a little metal pan. But once you understand how it works, it becomes an unshakable partner in your kitchen. This chapter is your no-fuss guide to mastering your bread machine from the inside out.

Understanding Your Bread Machine Settings

Most modern bread machines share similar core settings,

even if the names differ slightly by brand. You'll typically find buttons or dials for:

- **Basic or White Bread** – Your everyday loaf. Great for sandwich bread or plain white.

- **Whole Wheat** – Adjusts for the heavier flour by extending the knead and rise time.

- **Sweet** – Reduces bake temperature slightly to prevent sugar-heavy breads from overbrowning.

- **Dough Only** – Mixes and rises but doesn't bake. Use this for pizza, cinnamon rolls, or shaping by hand.

- **Rapid/Rapid Bake** – Shortens time. Handy, but can yield denser loaves.

- **Gluten-Free** – If available, this adjusts for flour blends that don't require kneading strength.

- **Crust Control** – Light, medium, or dark. Just a browning setting for the final stage.

Don't worry if your model doesn't have every setting listed. The recipes in this book are built around standard functions that work on almost any machine.

Pro Tip: Write your favorite cycles on a sticky note and tape it to your machine. Saves you from guessing later.

Yeast 101: Instant, Active Dry, or Bread Machine Yeast?

Bread baking begins with yeast—the tiny organisms that make your dough rise and create that fluffy, airy texture. But which one should you use?

- **Instant Yeast (a.k.a. Rapid-Rise or Bread Machine Yeast)**

This yeast is finely granulated and doesn't need to be dissolved in water. It can be mixed directly into the flour. It's the most reliable for bread machines and used in almost every recipe in this book.

- **Active Dry Yeast**

Slightly coarser and often requires proofing in warm water first. That step is not ideal for bread machines unless your machine specifically calls for it.

- **Fresh Yeast (Cake Yeast)**

Not recommended for bread machines. Too sensitive and short-lived.

Whenever possible, stick **to instant or bread machine yeast**—it gives consistent results and matches the machine's timing perfectly.

Storage Tip: Keep your yeast in an airtight container in the fridge or freezer. It can last 4–6 months without losing strength.

Flour 101: Choose the Right One

Your bread's flavor and structure depend heavily on the

flour you choose. Here's a breakdown:

- **Bread Flour**

Has higher protein (gluten) content. This gives bread structure and chew. It's ideal for sandwich loaves, whole grain, and any bread where you want that nice rise and elastic feel.

- **All-Purpose Flour**

Slightly lower protein but still works well, especially for softer loaves, sweet breads, or rolls. Some bakers use it exclusively.

- **Whole Wheat Flour**

Denser, more flavorful, and rich in fiber. Needs more liquid. Usually combined with bread flour for balance.

- **Gluten-Free Flours**

Require blends and specific recipes. Don't substitute directly.

- **Specialty Flours (Rye, Spelt, Oat, etc.)**

These add character but often need to be combined with bread flour to avoid dense results.

Golden Rule: Start with **bread flour or a mix of bread and all-purpose**, and only experiment once you're comfortable with the machine.

Layering Ingredients the Right Way

When using a bread machine, **the order matters**—and it's different from hand baking. That's because the machine starts mixing immediately, and you want to avoid premature yeast activation.

Here's the standard layering method (from bottom to top):

1. **Liquids first** – Water, milk, eggs, oils.
2. **Fats** – Butter or oils if not included in the liquid.
3. **Sugars and salt** – Separate them; salt can weaken yeast if placed directly on it.

4. **Flours** – Create a barrier between wet ingredients and yeast.

5. **Yeast last** – Always place it on top of the flour mound.

If you're using a **delay timer,** this step becomes crucial. You don't want your yeast to activate too early and collapse before baking even starts.

Add-ins (like nuts or raisins) are usually added after the first mix. Most machines beep when it's time to toss them in—listen for it!

Top 5 Beginner Mistakes to Avoid

Let's save you some heartache. These are the most common mistakes new bread machine users make:

1. Wrong Yeast

Active dry yeast in a machine often fails to rise properly. Use instant or bread machine yeast instead.

2. Mixing Up the Order

Putting yeast on the bottom or letting salt touch it directly can prevent the rise.

3. Too Much Flour

Packing your measuring cup can ruin hydration. Lightly spoon flour into the cup and level it off.

4. Opening the Lid Midway

Avoid lifting the lid during rising or baking stages. It lets out heat and can collapse the dough.

5. Ignoring the Dough in First 10 Minutes

Peek in after it starts kneading. If it looks too dry or too wet, adjust with a tablespoon of water or flour.

Bonus Tip: Your dough during kneading should form a smooth, slightly tacky ball—not wet and sticky, and not dry and crumbly.

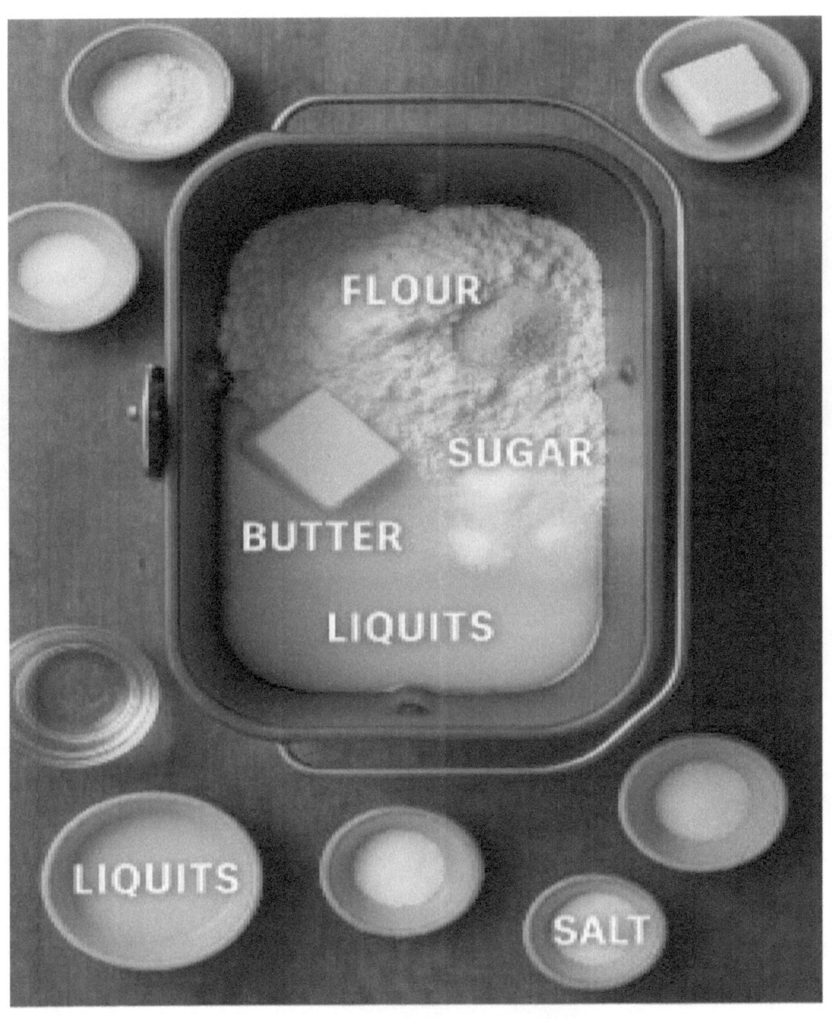

Mastering your machine is the difference between guessing and knowing. Once this chapter becomes second nature, the rest of this book becomes pure joy. From here on out, the recipes will guide your hands—but this chapter gives you the why, so you can trust your intuition, your machine, and your bread.

Let's bake smarter from here forward.

Chapter 2

5-Ingredient Everyday Breads

In a world overflowing with complex recipes and specialty ingredients, there's something beautifully grounding about simplicity. Just five ingredients. That's all it takes to fill your home with the smell of fresh, homemade bread. Not twenty. Not ten. Just five.

In this chapter, we strip bread down to its essence—flour, liquid, yeast, salt, and one magical extra that transforms it into something memorable. These are your go-to, no-fail, weekday workhorse loaves—made to be tossed into the bread machine and forgotten until your kitchen fills with the scent of home.

No fuss. No stress. Just deeply satisfying, rustic, everyday breads that anyone can make and everyone will remember.

Classic White Loaf

Soft, fluffy, and endlessly versatile—this is the everyday sandwich bread your grandmother would've sworn by.

Ingredients:

- Bread flour
- Water
- Salt
- Instant yeast
- Butter

Flavor Tip: Add a pinch of sugar if you want a slightly sweeter, more golden crust. It's optional—but lovely.

Texture: Light crumb, tender crust, perfect for slicing and toasting.

Best For: Sandwiches, grilled cheese, or slathering with jam and butter straight out of the toaster.

Honey Wheat

Slightly sweet, earthy, and nourishing—this loaf brings wholesome flavor without any heaviness.

Ingredients:

- Whole wheat flour
- Water
- Salt
- Instant yeast
- Honey

Make-It-Yours: *You can swap half the whole wheat for bread flour if you want a lighter crumb.*

Texture: *Moist, tender, and slightly dense—but still sliceable for everyday use.*

Best For: *Peanut butter toast, breakfast toast, turkey sandwiches.*

Rosemary Olive Oil

This loaf is a little more indulgent—fragrant with rosemary and rich from the olive oil. It's the one you serve with soup or alongside a cheese board when friends come over.

Ingredients:

- Bread flour
- Warm water
- Salt
- Instant yeast
- Olive oil (plus fresh or dried rosemary)

Aromatics Tip: Rub the rosemary between your palms before adding it—it releases the oils and deepens the flavor.

Texture: Crusty on the outside, soft and chewy inside.

Best For: *Dipping in soups, pairing with stews, or toasting with garlic butter.*

Cinnamon Swirl

Just five ingredients and you've got dessert—or at least breakfast that tastes like it should be dessert. Warm, sweet, and perfect for French toast.

Ingredients:

- Bread flour

- Milk or water

- Salt

- Instant yeast

- Cinnamon sugar blend (counted as one ingredient)

Assembly Tip: *For a dramatic swirl, use the dough cycle only. After it rises, roll it out by hand, spread the cinnamon-sugar, roll it back up and place it in a loaf pan. Bake in the oven for best results.*

Texture: Soft, *pull-apart crumb with a molten, sweet swirl inside.*

Best For: *French toast, sweet breakfast, gifting during the holidays.*

Cheese & Herb

The savory sibling of the cinnamon swirl, this loaf is punchy, cheesy, and rustic. Great with pasta or eaten on its own.

Ingredients:

- Bread flour
- Water or milk
- Salt
- Instant yeast
- Shredded cheddar (or cheese of choice)

Add-On Option: *A pinch of dried oregano, basil, or Italian* *seasoning gives it a pizza bread vibe.*

Texture: *Moist inside with gooey pockets of cheese and a golden, savory crust.*

Best For: *Slicing thick and warm, dipping in marinara, or eating straight from the cutting board.*

What Makes These Recipes Work?

Each loaf in this chapter follows the same reliable formula:

- **Flour + Liquid + Salt + Yeast + Flavor**

This lets you get into a baking rhythm where you don't need to relearn the process every time. You simply swap the flavor layer and you've got a whole new loaf.

That's the beauty of 5-ingredient breads—**they teach you how to trust your hands and your machine,** while still allowing for exploration. You'll start with these basics, and soon you'll be customizing your own signature loaves with confidence.

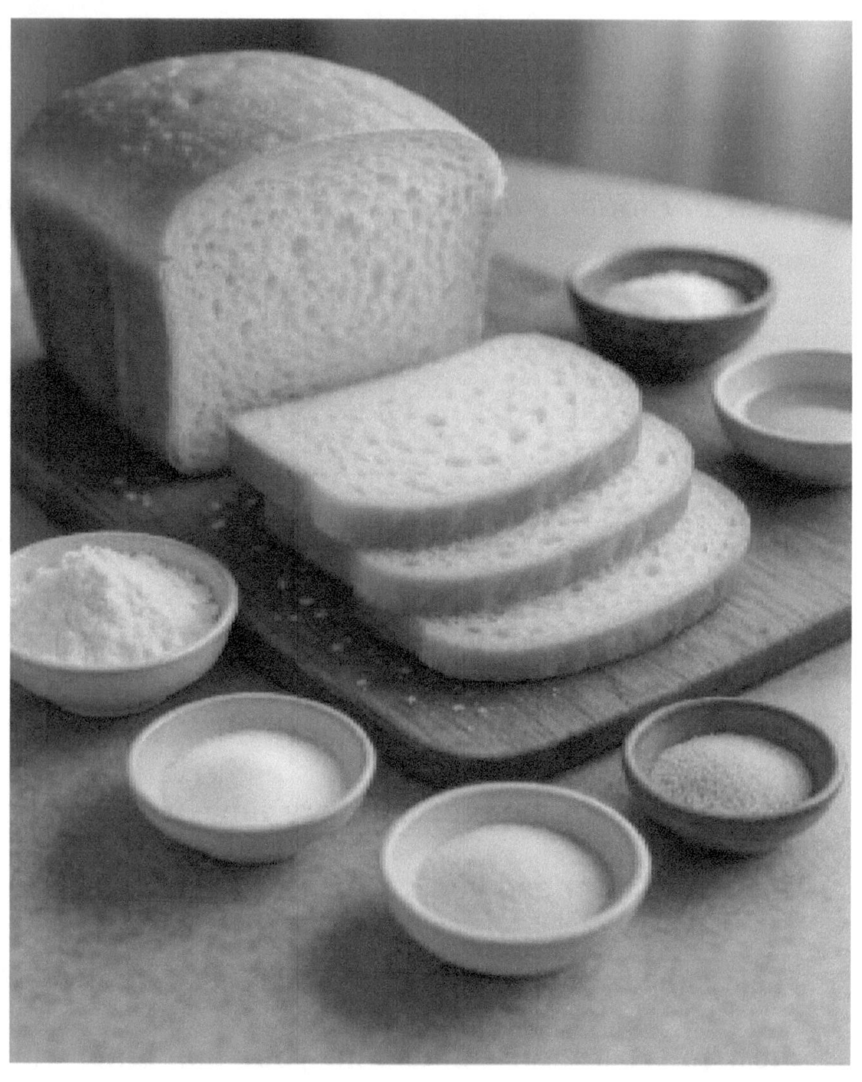

42

Chapter 3

Whole Grain & High-Fiber Breads

Whole grain bread has long been misunderstood as dense, dry, or reserved only for the ultra-health-conscious. But when done right—especially in a bread machine—it's none of those things. It's hearty, earthy, slightly nutty, and completely satisfying. These loaves don't just fill your belly—they fuel your day, feed your gut, and help stabilize your energy in ways that white bread never could.

And the best part? You don't need a bakery's skill set or a nutritionist's degree to bake them. Just a few nourishing ingredients, a button on your machine, and a little trust in the process.

This chapter features fiber-forward loaves that blend grains, seeds, and natural sweetness, proving that healthy bread can be just as delicious as the classic stuff—maybe even more so.

7-Grain Seed Bread

Rustic, nutty, and full of texture—this is the bread you slice thick, toast golden, and top with avocado or almond butter.

Core Ingredients:

- Bread flour
- Multigrain hot cereal mix or 7-grain blend (uncooked)
- Water or milk
- Instant yeast
- Salt

Optional Add-ins: *Sesame seeds, sunflower seeds, pumpkin seeds, or hemp hearts.*

Make-It-Yours Tip: *Soak the grains in warm water for 15–20 minutes before starting. This softens their texture and* *keeps the loaf moist.*

Best For: *Toasting, topping with hummus or mashed banana, sandwiching hearty vegetables or roasted meats.*

Oatmeal Raisin Bread

Soft and subtly sweet, this loaf has the heart of a muffin and the soul of Sunday morning. Perfect with coffee or tea.

Core Ingredients:

- Old-fashioned oats
- Whole wheat flour
- Water or milk
- Salt
- Raisins

Flavor Tip: *Add a dash of cinnamon or nutmeg if you like spice. A tablespoon of honey makes it slightly sweeter.*

Texture: *Chewy and soft with pops of sweetness from the* *raisins.*

Best For: *Breakfast toast, tea-time snacks, or warmed with a pat of salted butter.*

Flax & Chia Bread

High in omega-3s and fiber, this loaf feels light but satisfies like a protein bar. It's clean-eating bread with zero sacrifice.

Core Ingredients:

- Bread flour
- Ground flaxseed
- Chia seeds
- Warm water
- Salt

Hydration Tip: *Let the chia sit in warm water for 5–10 minutes before adding. It will form a gel-like texture that keeps the loaf moist and springy.*

Best For: *Toast with nut butter, egg sandwiches, or sliced thin for dipping into olive oil.*

Sprouted Wheat Bread

This is your back-to-basics, old-world-style loaf that feels nourishing from the first bite to the last. Earthy, slightly sweet, and rich in enzymes.

Core Ingredients:

- Sprouted whole wheat flour
- Water
- Salt
- Honey or molasses
- Instant yeast

Make-It-Yours: *Add a tablespoon of olive oil for a softer crust or a sprinkle of oats on top for visual appeal.*

Best For: *Thick slices with savory spreads, egg salad sandwiches, or avocado toast.*

Quinoa Loaf

Mild, slightly nutty, and delightfully chewy—this loaf turns the ancient grain into something fresh and modern.

Core Ingredients:

- Bread flour
- Cooked quinoa (cooled)
- Water
- Salt
- Instant yeast

Texture Boost: Rinse your quinoa thoroughly before cooking to avoid bitterness. The cooked grains add texture and moisture.

Best For: Cold-cut sandwiches, veggie-packed open-faced toasts, or as a base for grain-forward paninis.

The Magic of Fiber-Rich Loaves

These breads are more than recipes—they're part of a lifestyle shift. Baking with whole grains supports:

- **Digestive health**

- **Balanced blood sugar**

- **Satiety (feeling full longer)**

- **Heart health**

- **Sustained energy without spikes or crashes**

And thanks to the bread machine, making them is as simple as combining ingredients and pressing start. No kneading, no worrying—just clean, functional nourishment with the flavor of something slow and intentional.

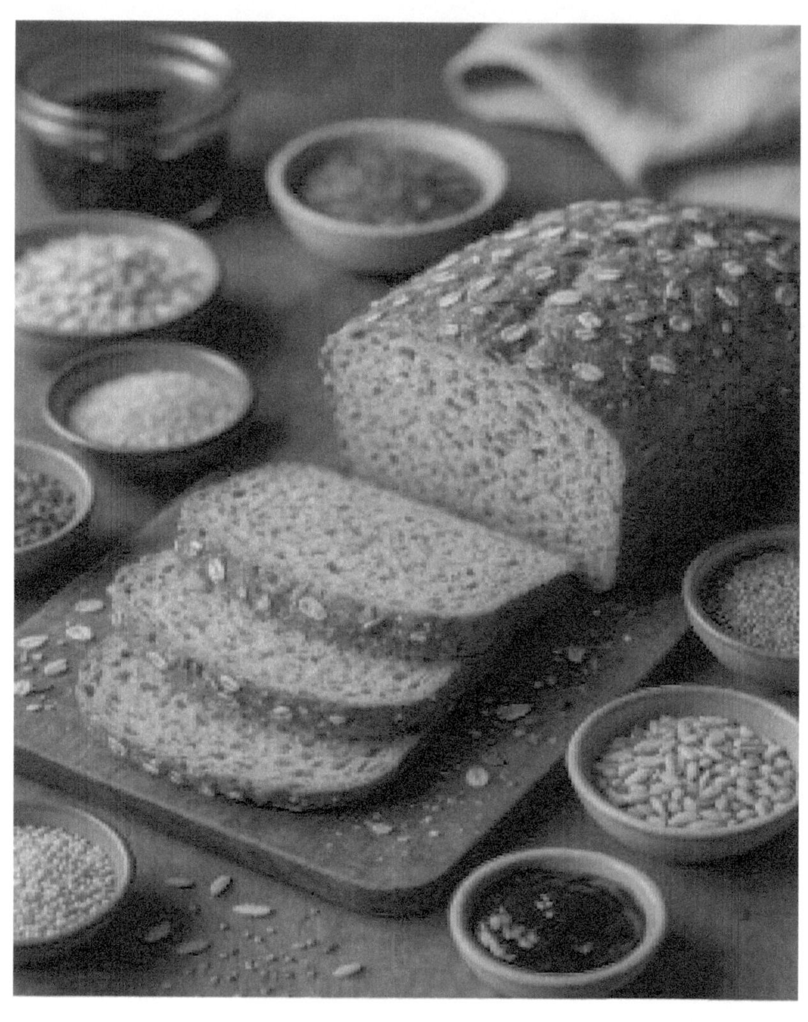

Chapter 4

Gluten-Free Goodness

Gluten-free bread has a reputation—and not always a good one. Too crumbly. Too dry. Too heavy. Too expensive.

But here's the truth: when you understand the why behind gluten-free baking and use the right combinations of ingredients, tools, and timing, you can create loaves that rival anything with wheat. **Yes, even in your bread machine.**

This chapter is for everyone who thought gluten-free bread had to be a compromise. It doesn't. With the right recipes and a few tricks, it becomes a celebration of texture, nutrition, and real comfort food—without the gluten.

Rice Flour Sandwich Bread

Light, neutral, and gently chewy—this is your go-to white sandwich bread, minus the gluten.

Core Ingredients:

- White rice flour
- Tapioca starch or potato starch
- Eggs or flax eggs
- Oil or melted butter
- Salt

Texture Tip: *Add a teaspoon of apple cider vinegar and a tablespoon of psyllium husk or xanthan gum to help bind the dough and mimic gluten's stretch.*

Best For: *PB&J sandwiches, morning toast, or grilled cheese.*

Almond Meal Honey Bread

Nutty, slightly sweet, and golden—this loaf is packed with healthy fats and natural moisture.

Core Ingredients:

- Almond flour or almond meal
- Eggs
- Baking powder or baking soda
- Honey
- Salt

Moisture Tip: *Almond flour bakes beautifully but can brown quickly. Use the "light crust" setting or remove a few minutes early.*

Best For: *Slicing warm with butter, topping with berries, or toasting for breakfast with tahini.*

Coconut Flour Loaf

A compact, slightly sweet loaf with incredible fiber and flavor. A little goes a long way with coconut flour.

Core Ingredients:

- Coconut flour
- Eggs (must use real eggs for structure)
- Oil or ghee
- Baking soda
- Salt

Warning: Coconut flour is ultra-absorbent. You'll use far less than other flours and need lots of moisture. Always let the batter sit for 5–10 minutes before baking so it fully hydrates.

Best For: Toasting with jam, spreading with nut butter, or serving alongside curries and stews.

Gluten-Free Multigrain Bread

A hearty, sliceable bread packed with grains and seeds—chewy, flavorful, and wonderfully satisfying.

Core Ingredients:

- Gluten-free flour blend (with rice flour, sorghum, or millet)
- Ground flax or psyllium husk
- Eggs or aquafaba
- Oil
- Salt

Add-Ins: Sunflower seeds, chia seeds, oats (certified gluten-free), sesame seeds

Best For: Sandwiches, toast, or pairing with soup. Keeps beautifully in the fridge.

Tips to Prevent Dry, Crumbly Textures in Gluten-

Free Bread Machine Baking

1. Use a Binding Agent

Always include one of the following: psyllium husk, xanthan gum, ground chia, or flaxseed meal. These mimic gluten's structure and help hold moisture.

2. Let the Batter Sit Before Baking

Unlike wheat dough, gluten-free bread "batter" is often more like cake batter. Letting it rest allows the flours to hydrate, giving a more cohesive texture.

3. Add Moisture-Rich Ingredients

Yogurt, applesauce, mashed banana, or even just more fat (like avocado oil or olive oil) helps prevent dryness.

4. Don't Over-Bake

Gluten-free breads dry out faster. If your machine doesn't let you control bake time, check it early and remove if needed.

5. Storage Matters

Gluten-free bread can dry out quickly. Wrap tightly and store in the fridge for 3–5 days, or slice and freeze for longer shelf life.

6. Use the Right Cycle

If your machine has a "gluten-free" setting—use it. If not, use the "quick bread" or "cake" cycle, which skips the punch-down phase (that can deflate GF batters).

Why This Chapter Matters

Gluten-free eaters often feel left out of the joy of baking bread. This chapter gives it back to them—with results that taste like love, not restriction. And whether you eat gluten-free by necessity or by choice, these recipes let you say yes to warmth, yes to nourishment, and yes to the smell of bread baking in your home.

Because everyone deserves that.

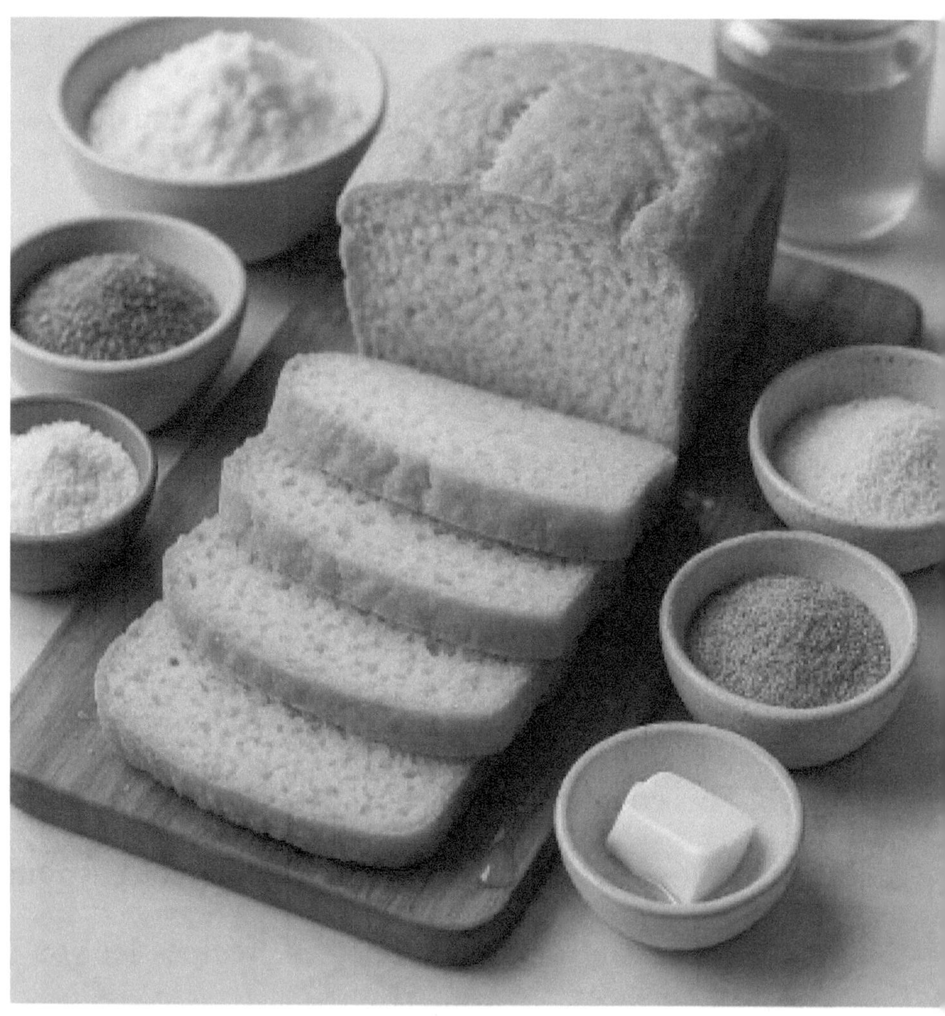

Chapter 5

Sweet Breads & Breakfast Loaves

There's something special about a kitchen that smells like bananas, cinnamon, or melted chocolate. These aren't just loaves—they're invitations. To slow down. To brew a cup of coffee. To sit at the table a little longer.

In this chapter, you'll find **sweet breads and breakfast loaves** that come together effortlessly in the bread machine but taste like you spent all morning baking. These are the recipes that make weekends feel like holidays and weekdays feel like you've paused time—if only for a slice.

They're also a perfect introduction to baking for loved ones: less fuss, fewer bowls, and always a guaranteed smile.

Banana Walnut Bread

Moist, golden, and dotted with crunchy walnuts—this is the comfort loaf you'll want to make every week.

Core Ingredients:

- Ripe mashed bananas
- Bread flour or all-purpose flour
- Brown sugar or coconut sugar
- Eggs
- Chopped walnuts

Flavor Notes: Add a dash of cinnamon or vanilla if you like it extra cozy.

Texture: Dense and rich with soft banana pockets and nutty crunch.

Best For: Breakfast, dessert, or as a warm gift for someone who needs a little love.

__Pro Tip:__ Use the "quick bread" or "cake" setting. Banana bread batter is more like cake than dough.

Lemon Blueberry Loaf

Bright, fragrant, and bursting with juicy berries—this loaf is like springtime in a slice.

Core Ingredients:

- All-purpose flour
- Eggs
- Lemon juice + zest
- Fresh or frozen blueberries
- Sugar

__Make-It-Yours:__ Swap in almond flour for part of the AP flour for a nuttier profile. Glaze with lemon icing if serving for brunch.

Texture: *Light and fluffy with blueberry bursts throughout.*

Best For: *Weekend mornings, garden brunches, or afternoon tea.*

Chocolate Chip Brioche

Soft, buttery, and studded with semi-sweet chocolate chips—this is the grown-up answer to chocolate cravings.

Core Ingredients:

- Bread flour
- Eggs
- Butter
- Sugar
- Chocolate chips

Richness Tip: *Let butter come fully to room temp. Cold butter affects the brioche's delicate rise.*

Texture: *Soft pull-apart crumb with melted chocolate in every bite.*

Best For: *French toast, dessert with coffee, or sneaking a slice before bed.*

Apple Cinnamon Swirl

A golden crust hides a gooey cinnamon-apple ribbon that feels like a warm hug on a cold morning.

Core Ingredients:

- Bread flour or all-purpose flour
- Chopped apples (peeled)
- Cinnamon sugar
- Butter
- Eggs or milk

Layer Tip: *Use the dough cycle, then roll out and fill with apples + cinnamon before baking in a loaf pan for the most beautiful swirl.*

Texture: *Tender crumb with sweet spiced layers and fruit pockets.*

Best For: *Toasting with butter, pairing with chai tea, or baking on Sundays.*

Sticky Raisin Tea Bread

This loaf is deeply flavorful—dark, sweet, and just sticky enough to feel like a treat. Inspired by classic tea loaves from the UK.

Core Ingredients:

- All-purpose or whole wheat flour
- Brewed black tea (cooled)
- Raisins or currants
- Brown sugar
- Baking powder or yeast (depending on cycle)

Moisture Trick: *Soak the raisins in the tea before adding for max plumpness and flavor.*

__Texture:__ Dense but moist, with caramel undertones and a sticky crust.

__Best For:__ Slicing thin with butter, sharing with friends, or serving with hot tea on rainy afternoons.

The Sweet Simplicity of Bread Machine Baking

What makes these loaves special isn't just the flavor—it's the ease. While traditional sweet breads might need multiple bowls, hand-kneading, and oven babysitting, your bread machine does the work quietly, reliably, and beautifully.

All you need to do is measure, load, press start… and let the aroma do the rest.

And once you've made these once, you'll come back to them again and again. Not because you have to—but because you want to. Because they make the ordinary feel extraordinary.

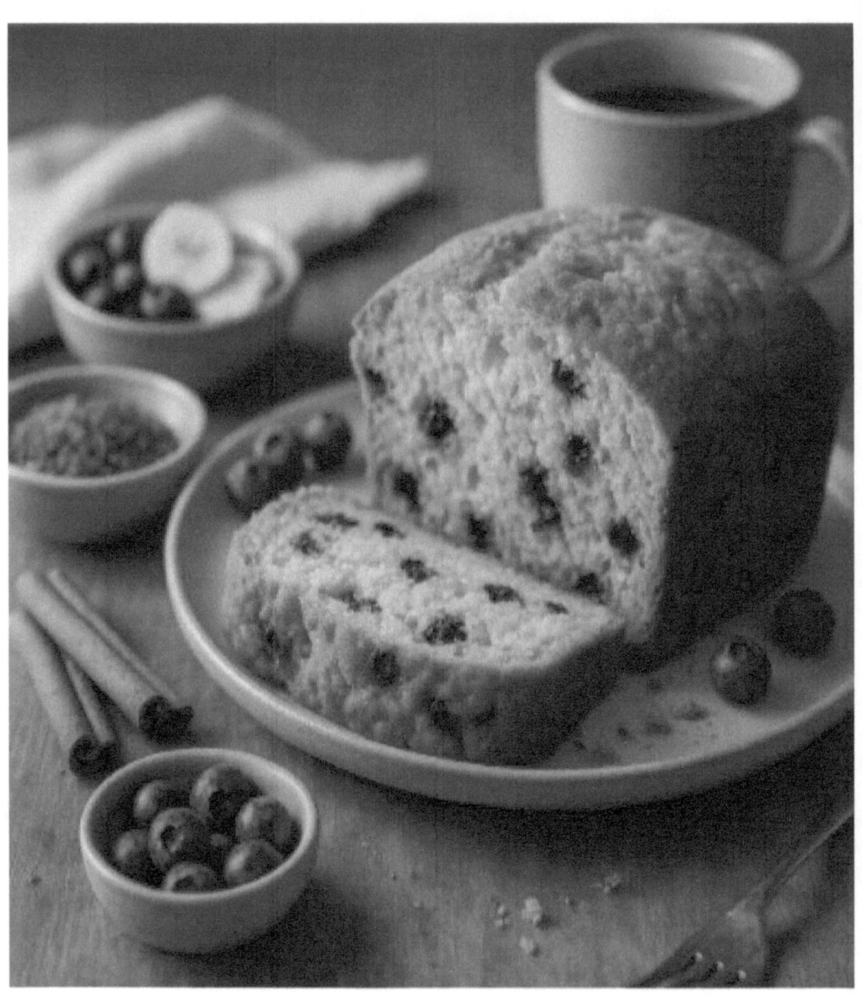

Chapter 6

Savory, Herby & Cheese Breads

Not every bread needs to be sweet, soft, or safe. Some should be bold. Some should make your mouth water before you've even sliced into them. Some are meant for pairing with soup, stuffing with deli meats, or pulling apart at the center of the table with friends and family.

This chapter is for those breads—the savory loaves, where garlic, cheddar, herbs, and spice meet the warmth of home baking. Every recipe is tested for the bread machine, but made to feel like something out of a cozy farmhouse oven.

If you love crusty tops, melted cheese, and flavor that hits your nose before it hits your tongue, these loaves are your new go-to.

Jalapeño Cheddar Bread

Sharp, spicy, and unapologetically bold. This loaf brings the heat and the cheese.

Core Ingredients:

- Bread flour
- Sharp cheddar (shredded)
- Jalapeños (diced, fresh or pickled)
- Milk or water
- Salt

Flavor Tip: Remove jalapeño seeds for mild heat, or leave them in for that true firebread experience.

Texture: Moist, cheesy crumb with crisp golden edges and pepper pockets.

Best For: Grilled cheese with a kick, chili night, or snacking warm from the slicer.

Garlic Parmesan Bread

Rich, garlicky, and crowned with a crust of melted parmesan—this one makes your kitchen smell like heaven.

Core Ingredients:

- Bread flour

- Parmesan (grated)

- Garlic (minced or powder)

- Butter or olive oil

- Salt

Aromatics Tip: Use roasted garlic for a sweeter, more mellow flavor, or garlic powder for convenience.

Texture: Fluffy inside with a cheesy, slightly crisp top.

Best For: Pasta dinners, dipping in marinara, or slicing thick for garlic bread.

Sun-Dried Tomato & Basil Loaf

Bright, earthy, and Italian-inspired—this loaf is the definition of rustic charm.

Core Ingredients:

- Bread flour or a mix of white + whole wheat
- Sun-dried tomatoes (chopped, oil-packed preferred)
- Fresh or dried basil
- Olive oil
- Salt

Sun-Dried Tip: Pat tomatoes dry if using oil-packed to avoid soggy pockets in the crumb.

Texture: Chewy and flavorful with herby specks and tomato richness.

Best For: Sandwiches with mozzarella, slicing for bruschetta, or serving alongside antipasto.

Dill Pickle Bread

Surprisingly addictive—tangy, briny, and herbaceous. A true conversation starter at any table.

Core Ingredients:

- Bread flour
- Dill pickles (chopped)
- Pickle juice (as liquid)
- Dried dill or fresh
- Salt

Flavor Tip: A splash of pickle juice in place of water adds zing and keeps the loaf extra moist.

Texture: Soft inside with herb-flecked crust and the unmistakable scent of dill.

Best For: Ham and cheese sandwiches, burger buns, or served warm with cream cheese.

Ranch-Seasoned Pull-Apart Bread

Fun, family-friendly, and loaded with herby flavor—this is the ultimate comfort bread.

Core Ingredients:

- Bread flour
- Ranch seasoning (store-bought or homemade)
- Cheddar or mozzarella
- Butter
- Salt

Make It Pull-Apart: *Use the "dough" cycle. After rising, cut into small pieces, roll in melted butter + seasoning, layer in a loaf or bundt pan, and bake in the oven.*

Texture: *Gooey, cheesy, buttery layers you can tear apart piece by piece.*

Best For: *Game day, potlucks, or anytime you're feeding a hungry crowd.*

Savory Breads, Simple Moments

These breads aren't just side dishes—they're centerpieces. Perfect for dunking, layering, stuffing, or eating straight from the board. They remind us that bread can be indulgent, playful, and deeply satisfying without being complicated.

And with your bread machine, these big flavors come with almost no effort—just ingredients, a press of a button, and a little anticipation.

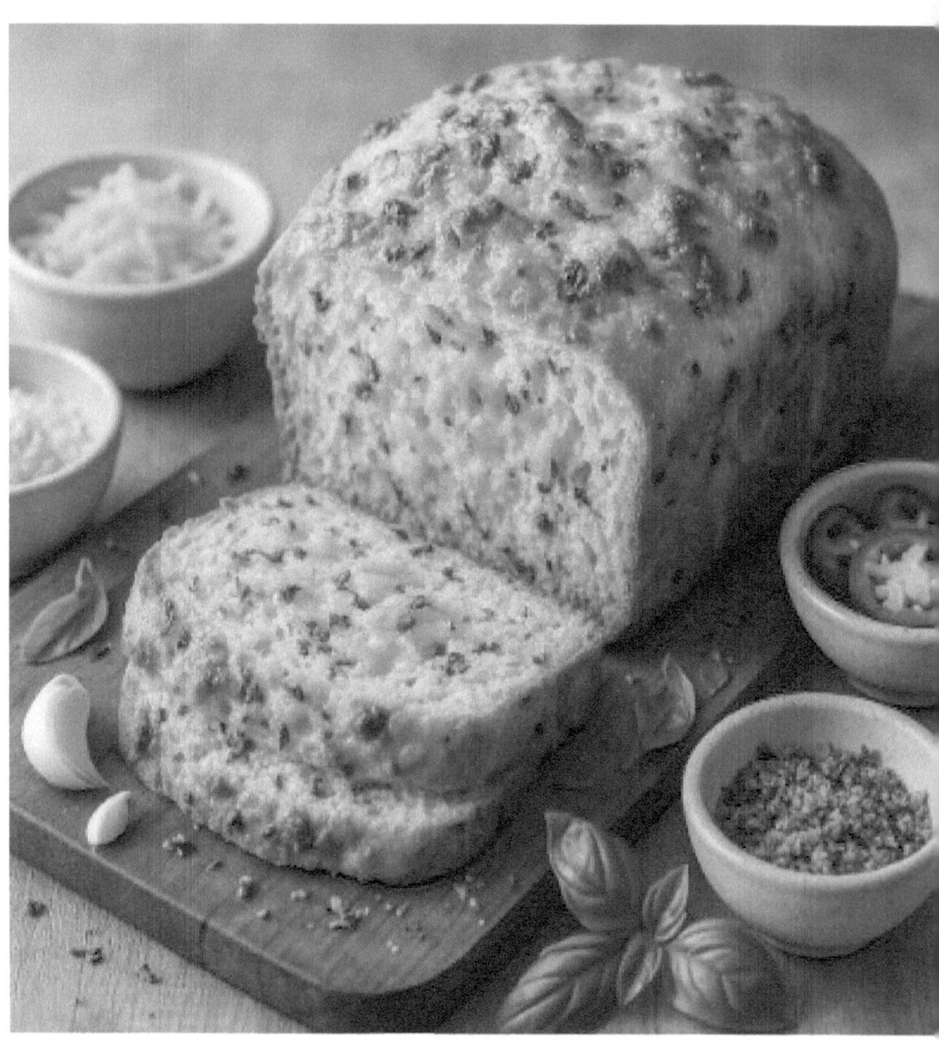

Chapter 7

Rolls, Buns & Sandwich Starters

There's something deeply inviting about bread you can pull apart with your hands. Rolls that steam when torn. Buns that cradle burgers or breakfast sandwiches. Doughs that twist into something beautiful and unforgettable.

In this chapter, we step away from the traditional loaf and into the world of shaped breads—doughs that begin in your bread machine and come to life in your hands. These recipes use the "dough" cycle, giving you all the magic of kneading and rising without the mess. From soft pillowy rolls to golden focaccia, every bake is beginner-friendly, make-ahead friendly, and guaranteed to impress.

Soft Dinner Rolls

Fluffy, golden, and lightly sweet—these classic rolls melt

in your mouth and disappear fast.

Core Ingredients:

- Bread flour
- Warm milk
- Butter
- Sugar
- Instant yeast

Shaping Tip: After the dough cycle, divide into 12–16 balls, roll smooth, and arrange in a greased baking dish. Let rise until puffy, then bake at 350°F until golden.

Texture: Soft inside with a light crust—perfect for pulling apart.

Best For: Holiday dinners, soup sides, or slathering with honey butter.

Onion Burger Buns

Bold and savory with a touch of sweetness from caramelized onion—these buns hold their shape and their flavor.

Core Ingredients:

- Bread flour
- Warm water
- Olive oil or butter
- Caramelized onions (finely chopped)
- Salt

Shape & Finish: After the dough cycle, form into 6–8 flat rounds, press slightly, and sprinkle with sesame or onion flakes. Bake at 375°F until browned.

Texture: Chewy but tender with a rich, savory aroma.

Best For: Sandwiches, pulled pork sliders, grilled veggie stacks.

Herb Focaccia

Crusty edges, pillowy middle, and deeply infused with herbs and olive oil—this is a showstopper made simple.

Core Ingredients:

- Bread flour
- Warm water
- Olive oil (liberally!)
- Dried or fresh herbs (rosemary, thyme, oregano)
- Sea salt

Method: *After dough cycle, press into a greased pan, dimple with fingers, drizzle with oil, and sprinkle with herbs. Bake at 425°F until golden.*

Texture: *Crisp bottom, airy interior, rich in flavor.*

Best For: *Dipping in olive oil, serving with soup or salad, or eating straight off the pan.*

Bagel-Style Dough (For Boiling & Baking)

Chewy, dense, and satisfying—these bagels start in your machine and finish with a quick boil + bake.

Core Ingredients:

- Bread flour

- Warm water

- Sugar

- Salt

- Instant yeast

How-To: *After dough cycle, divide and shape into rings. Boil in sweetened water for 30 seconds per side, then bake at 425°F until glossy and golden.*

Add-ons: *Top with sesame, poppy, or "everything" seasoning.*

Best For: *Breakfast, sandwiches, or freezing for grab-and-go days.*

Cinnamon Roll Dough

A soft, buttery dough perfect for swirling into cinnamon rolls, sticky buns, or even braided coffee cakes.

Core Ingredients:

- All-purpose flour
- Warm milk
- Butter
- Sugar
- Instant yeast

Assembly: After dough cycle, roll into a rectangle, spread with cinnamon-sugar butter, roll up, slice, and bake in a dish. Glaze with cream cheese icing or vanilla glaze.

Texture: Pillow-soft with gooey centers and golden spirals.

Best For: Brunches, birthdays, or just because.

From Dough to Memory

There's something special about shaping bread with your hands. It slows you down. Connects you to something old and good. And even though the bread machine does the heavy lifting, **you bring the life into these loaves** with your shaping, rising, and finishing.

Whether you're serving a crowd or just want a fresh roll with dinner, this chapter gives you doughs that can do it all. Soft rolls. Bold buns. Flaky focaccia. Chewy bagels. Sweet spirals.

And every one of them starts the same way: with a machine, a button, and a little bit of dough.

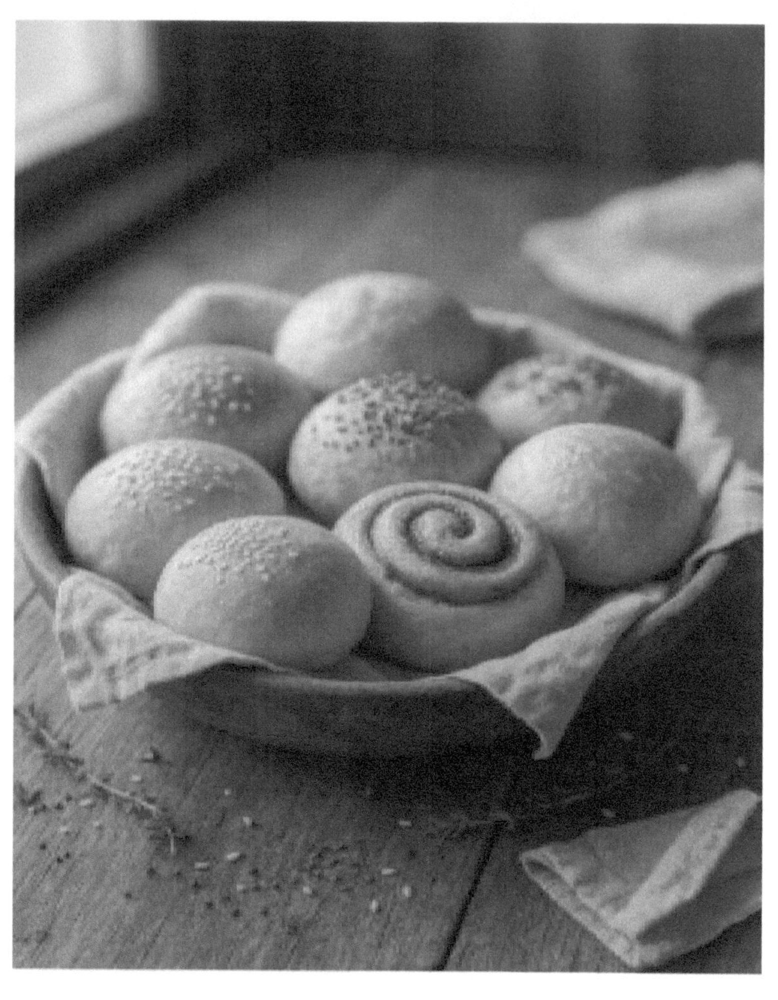

Chapter 8

International-Inspired Recipes

Bread is universal. Every culture has its own version—shaped by geography, climate, tradition, and taste. Some are crusty and rustic, others soft and enriched. But all are a reflection of something deeper: home.

In this chapter, we bring the world to your bread machine with recipes inspired by iconic international loaves. These are not exact replicas from artisanal bakeries in Paris or Tokyo, but carefully simplified versions that honor their roots—designed to work beautifully in your machine and connect you to a sense of place, story, and warmth.

IT Italian Ciabatta

Rustic, airy, and chewy—this famous Italian slipper bread is perfect for sandwiches or dipping in olive oil.

Core Ingredients:

- Bread flour
- Water
- Olive oil
- Salt
- Instant yeast

Texture Tip: *The dough should be very wet and sticky—this is what creates the signature air holes. Use the "dough" cycle, then bake on a sheet pan for best results.*

Best For: *Dipping in balsamic and olive oil, panini sandwiches, or tearing apart at the dinner table.*

FR French Pain de Mie

Soft, sweet, and elegant—pain de mie is the French version of sandwich bread, with a tender, fine crumb and a whisper of sweetness.

Core Ingredients:

- Bread flour

- Milk

- Butter

- Sugar

- Salt

Baking Tip: *Bake in a loaf pan with a lid if you have one to get its signature square shape.*

Texture: *Smooth, rich, and close-crumbed—great for slicing.*

Best For: *Breakfast toast, croque monsieur, or cucumber sandwiches.*

JP Japanese Milk Bread (Shokupan)

Incredibly soft, lightly sweet, and cloud-like—this loaf is a dream in texture and taste.

Core Ingredients:

- Bread flour

- Milk (or milk powder + water)

- Sugar

- Butter

- Tangzhong paste (flour cooked with water, optional but worth it)

Tangzhong Tip: For extra softness and longevity, cook a paste of 1 tbsp flour + 5 tbsp water until thickened, then let cool before mixing with the dough.

Texture: Pillow-soft with a springy bounce.

Best For: Toast, jam, sandwiches, or snacking plain.

RU Russian Black Bread

Dark, dense, and packed with depth—this bread is tangy, savory, and slightly sweet with undertones of rye and spice.

Core Ingredients:

- Rye flour + bread flour

- Molasses or dark honey

- Cocoa powder (just a hint)

- Caraway seeds or fennel

- Instant yeast

Flavor Depth: A touch of vinegar or instant coffee brings out that iconic tang.

Texture: Hearty and firm, best served sliced thin.

Best For: Smoked fish, cured meats, pickled vegetables, or bold cheeses.

IN Indian Masala Bread

Spiced, aromatic, and utterly comforting—this loaf combines warmth, herbs, and subtle heat in every bite.

Core Ingredients:

- Bread flour

- Warm milk or water

- Chopped green chilies (optional)

- Cilantro or curry leaves

- Indian spices (cumin, turmeric, garam masala)

Aromatics Tip: Sauté spices in a little oil before adding to dough for maximum flavor.

Texture: Soft and savory with flecks of herbs and color.

Best For: Serving with soups, stews, or using as a bold sandwich base.

Why Global Breads Belong on Your Table

Bread is one of the few foods every culture claims and cherishes. These loaves offer more than flavor, they offer perspective, reminding us that comfort, creativity, and nourishment are shared human desires.

And while they come from different kitchens across the world, today they come together in yours. Your bread machine is now a passport, and this chapter is your first-class ticket.

Bon voyage—and buon appetito.

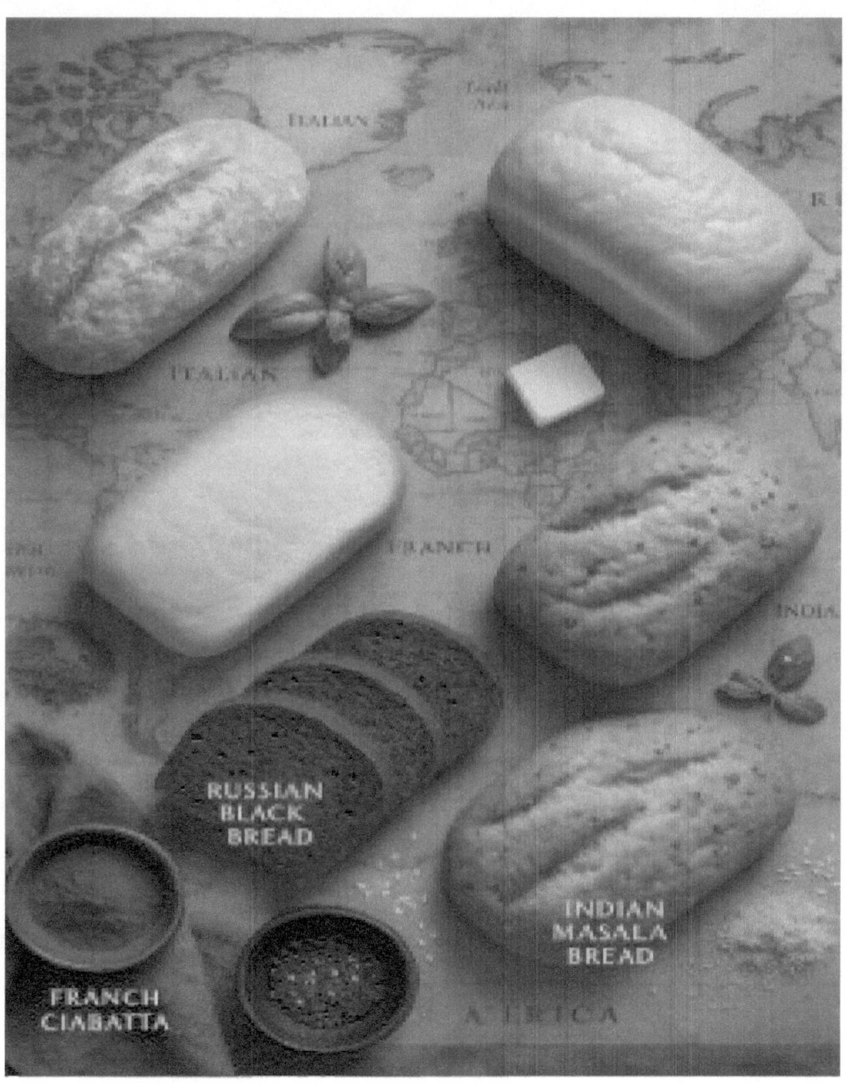

Chapter 9

Kid-Approved & Fun Recipes

There's a special kind of magic in baking with kids. Flour on their cheeks. Dough stuck to fingers. Giggles filling the kitchen. These aren't just recipes—they're invitations. To play. To learn. To connect.

In this chapter, we focus on fun, interactive, and picky-eater–friendly breads that children will love to make and eat. Whether it's a swirl of peanut butter and jelly, a rainbow of color in a soft loaf, or tiny animal shapes that come to life in the oven—every recipe here is about sparking curiosity and joy.

And don't worry—while the results look whimsical, every dough begins with the bread machine doing the heavy lifting.

Pizza Dough (Bread Machine Edition)

Stretchy, chewy, and ready for toppings—this dough turns any night into pizza night.

Core Ingredients:

- Bread flour

- Warm water

- Olive oil

- Sugar

- Instant yeast

Use: Set your machine to the "dough" cycle. Once it finishes, roll out and top with tomato sauce, cheese, and all the toppings your kids love.

Best For: Personal pizzas, pizza pinwheels, or cheesy breadsticks.

Kid Tip: Let kids make faces or shapes with toppings before baking.

PB&J Swirl Bread

Everything kids love in a sandwich—baked right into the loaf. Sweet, sticky, and irresistibly swirled.

Core Ingredients:

- Bread flour
- Milk or water
- Salt
- Peanut butter
- Fruit jam or preserves

Assembly: Use "dough" cycle. After rising, roll dough into a rectangle, spread PB&J, then roll up and place in a loaf pan. Bake at 350°F.

Texture: Soft and sweet, like a sandwich-meets-snack hybrid.

Best For: Lunchbox slices, after-school snacks, or breakfast with fruit.

Chocolate Marble Loaf

A bakery-style loaf with dramatic chocolate swirls and tender sweetness. It looks fancy, but it's easy.

Core Ingredients:

- All-purpose flour
- Cocoa powder + sugar (swirl)
- Butter
- Eggs
- Milk

Make-It-Magic: Use "dough" cycle. After rising, divide in half. Mix cocoa into one portion, layer, roll, and twist into loaf pan.

Texture: Cake-like, rich, and beautiful when sliced.

Best For: Birthday breakfasts, dessert toast, or weekend treats.

Rainbow Bread (With Natural Colors)

Vibrant and fun—this loaf uses natural ingredients for a colorful surprise that feels magical, not artificial.

Core Ingredients:

- Bread flour

- Warm water

- Butter

- Salt

- Natural colorings (e.g. beet juice, turmeric, spinach, blueberry puree)

How-To: *Use dough cycle, then divide into 4–5 sections. Color each, roll into ropes, stack, and braid or layer before baking.*

Texture: *Slightly sweet, fluffy, and show-stopping when sliced.*

Best For: *Birthday parties, lunchbox fun, or teaching kids about colors in nature.*

Mini Bread Animals (Shaped by Hand)

Whimsical little bears, turtles, bunnies, or hedgehogs made from soft dough. Almost too cute to eat.

Core Ingredients:

- All-purpose flour
- Milk
- Sugar
- Butter
- Instant yeast

Shaping Fun: *After dough cycle, divide and shape into animal forms using raisins, chocolate chips, or seeds for eyes. Bake until golden.*

Best For: *School lunches, playdates, or rainy day baking projects.*

Parent Tip: *Let kids create their own "bread pets"—it teaches measuring, patience, and builds confidence.*

Why This Chapter Matters

These recipes are more than playful. They're about building connection between you and your child, between your child and food, between messy hands and real life learning.

Kids who bake gain confidence, develop motor skills, and build memories that stick. And the best part? With your bread machine doing the groundwork, you get to say yes more often—to baking, to experimenting, to making something together.

These are the loaves they'll ask for again and again. And one day, they might bake them for their own kids.

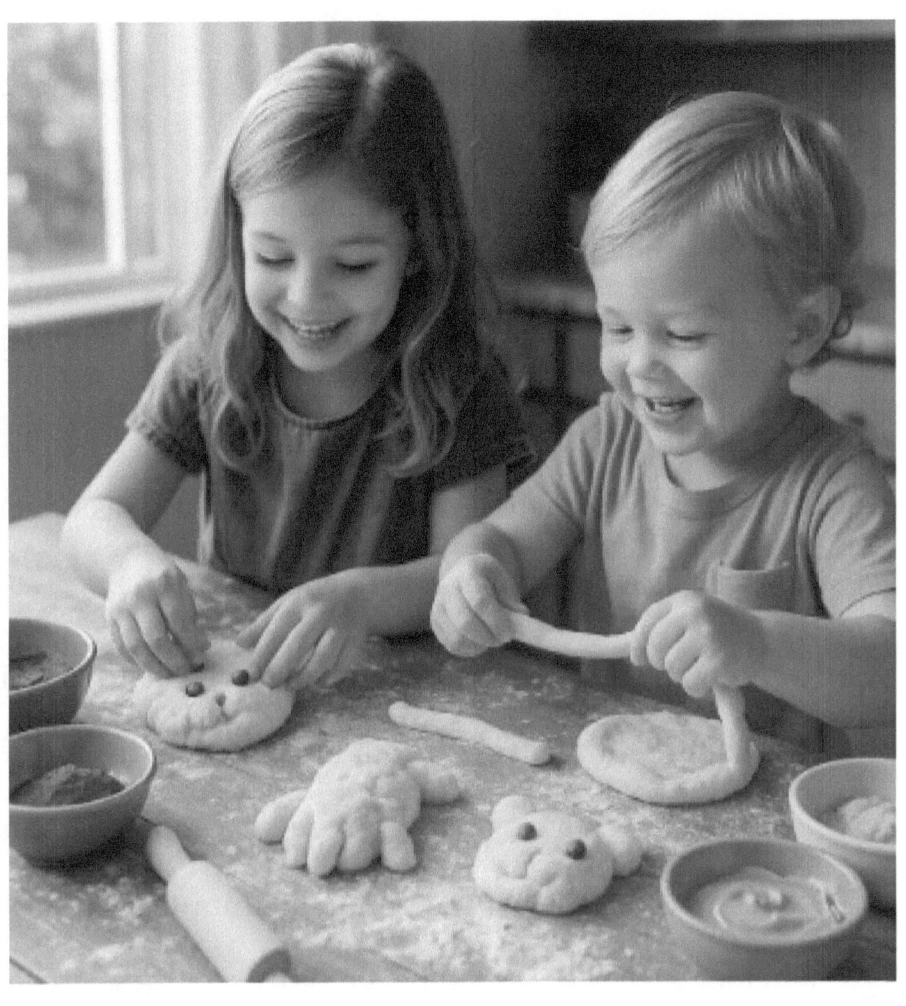

Chapter 10

Leftover Loaf Transformations

It happens. That last third of a loaf. A few too many slices left out overnight. The ends no one wants.

But in a baker's kitchen, nothing is ever truly wasted. Day-old bread is a beginning, not an end.

In this chapter, we transform humble leftovers into something unforgettable. From buttery croutons to gooey bread pudding, these recipes give new life to yesterday's loaves and often steal the spotlight from the fresh ones. Whether savory or sweet, baked or tossed, these creations close the loop with flavor and frugality.

Homemade Croutons

Crispy, golden cubes bursting with flavor—perfect for

tossing over soups or salads.

How-To:

- Cube leftover bread into 1-inch pieces.

- Toss with olive oil, garlic powder, salt, and herbs (like thyme or rosemary).

- Bake at 375°F for 15–20 minutes, flipping once.

Best With: *Caesar salad, creamy soups, or snacking straight from the tray.*

Pro Tip: *Use firmer loaves like ciabatta, sourdough, or multigrain for crunch.*

French Toast Casserole

A cozy, custard-soaked bake that's perfect for weekend mornings or holiday brunch.

Ingredients:

- Cubed bread (white, sweet, or milk bread work best)

- Eggs

- Milk or cream

- Vanilla

- Maple syrup

Optional: cinnamon, raisins, or fruit

Method: Soak bread cubes in egg mixture, pour into buttered dish, let sit 30 minutes (or overnight), and bake until golden and puffed.

Texture: *Soft and rich inside, lightly crisp on top.*

Best For: *Feeding a crowd or repurposing sweet loaves like banana or cinnamon swirl.*

Bread Pudding

Sweet, comforting, and endlessly customizable—bread pudding is proof that the best desserts come from humble roots.

Base Ingredients:

- Cubed bread (day-old, preferably sweet or neutral)
- Milk or cream
- Eggs
- Sugar
- Butter

Flavor Variations:

- Chocolate chip & orange zest
- Raisin & rum
- Apple & cinnamon
- Vanilla bean with caramel sauce

Method: Pour custard over bread, let soak, bake in a water bath for a silky finish.

Texture: Custard-soft inside, golden crust on top.

Best For: Dessert, warm breakfasts, or reheating through

the week.

Panzanella Salad

A vibrant, rustic salad that turns crusty bread into a Mediterranean feast.

Core Ingredients:

- Day-old bread chunks (preferably ciabatta or focaccia)
- Cherry tomatoes
- Red onions
- Cucumber
- Fresh basil
- Olive oil + red wine vinegar dressing

Method: Toast bread cubes lightly, toss with chopped veggies and dressing. Let sit for 20 minutes to soak up flavors.

Best For: *Summer meals, grilled meats, or as a light* *vegetarian main.*

Flavor Boost: *Add crumbled feta, capers, or grilled chicken.*

Garlic Toast Bites

Crisp, buttery, and bursting with garlic—these bites are dangerously snackable.

How-To:

- Slice or cube bread
- Melt butter with minced garlic, parsley, and salt
- Brush over bread, bake at 375°F until golden

Optional: *Top with shredded mozzarella, parmesan, or crushed red pepper.*

Best For: *Party trays, pasta night, or dipping in tomato soup.*

The Beauty of Bread That Comes Back

This chapter closes the loop in the most delicious way. It reminds us that **nothing in the kitchen needs to be wasted**—and often, the most comforting meals come from what we nearly threw away.

A stale loaf isn't a problem. It's potential. It's pudding, or croutons, or something your guests ask for again and again.

This is the heart of good home cooking: making the most of what we have, and loving it into something more.

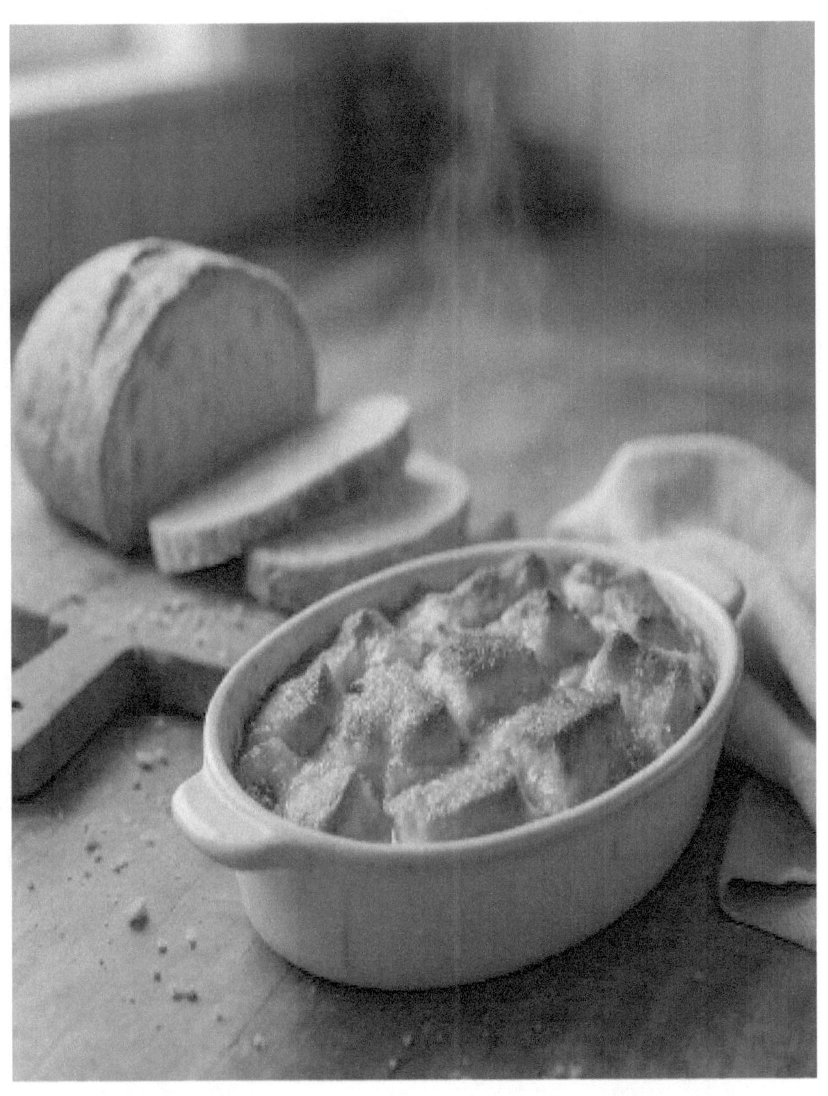

BONUS CHAPTER

Troubleshooting & Pro Tips

Even with the best intentions (and the best machine), things can go sideways in baking. A sunken loaf. A crust like concrete. A gummy center. It happens to all of us.

This chapter isn't just about fixing what went wrong—it's about understanding why it happened and how to get it right next time. Because breadmaking isn't just science—it's a relationship. And like any relationship, it improves with attention, patience, and a few inside tips.

Let's walk through the most common bread mishaps and how to avoid (or fix) them—with grace, not panic.

Why Did My Bread Collapse?

Collapsed bread usually looks like a loaf that rose

beautifully… and then sunk in the middle like a sad soufflé.

Possible Culprits:

- **Too much yeast or sugar** (causing over-rising)
- **Weak flour or low gluten content**
- **Overproofing** during the rise cycle
- **Lifting the lid** mid-bake or opening too early post-bake

Pro Tip: *Use bread flour for better structure. Stick to recipe proportions. Let the bread rest at least 10 minutes before slicing.*

Why Is My Bread Too Dense?

A dense, heavy loaf can feel like a brick—but it's almost always fixable with a few adjustments.

Causes:

- **Too much flour** or not enough liquid

- **Inactive yeast** (expired or killed by hot water)

- **Too little kneading** (resulting in poor gluten development)

Pro Tip: Check yeast freshness. Use warm—not hot—water (about 110°F). And if your machine has a "knead" or "rise" customization, experiment there.

Can I Save Undercooked Bread?

Yes! Don't toss it—rescue it.

What to Do:

- If it's just underdone in the middle: wrap in foil and bake in your oven at 350°F for 10–15 minutes.

- If it's gummy: slice and toast or use in recipes like croutons, stuffing, or bread pudding.

Pro Tip: *Always test doneness. Tap the bottom of the loaf—it should sound hollow. Or insert a thermometer: the interior should read at least* **190°F–200°F** *for most breads.*

Altitude, Weather & Flour Differences

Bread is moody. It changes based on where you live and what's in your pantry.

Altitude Tips:

- At higher elevations, reduce yeast slightly and increase liquid a bit.
- Use shorter rising times or colder liquids.

Humidity Effects:

- On humid days, flour can absorb moisture—start with a bit less liquid.
- In dry climates, you may need to add extra liquid gradually.

Flour Matters:

- Bread flour = strong gluten = better structure

- Whole wheat = heavier texture = often needs more moisture or a white flour blend

Pro Tip: Get to know your flour. Even different brands absorb differently. Measure by weight for better accuracy.

How to Clean and Store Your Bread Machine

Don't forget—your machine is the heart of the operation. Keep it in good shape and it will love you back.

Cleaning Tips:

- Always unplug before cleaning

- Wipe the inside and outside with a damp cloth (no submerging)

- Never immerse the pan or heating unit

- Remove stuck dough gently—never scrape with metal

Storing Tips:

- Store with lid open to avoid moisture buildup

- Keep the pan and kneading blade dry and separate if needed

- If you bake infrequently, cover with a cloth or store in a clean box

Pro Tip: *Keep a dedicated small brush or wooden skewer handy for cleaning around the kneading paddle and pan corners.*

Final Thought: Every Baker Makes Mistakes

It's not about being perfect. It's about staying curious. Trying again. Adjusting one small thing and watching a loaf go from "meh" to "marvelous."

Your bread machine is a tool. But you are the baker. And this chapter? It's your secret weapon.

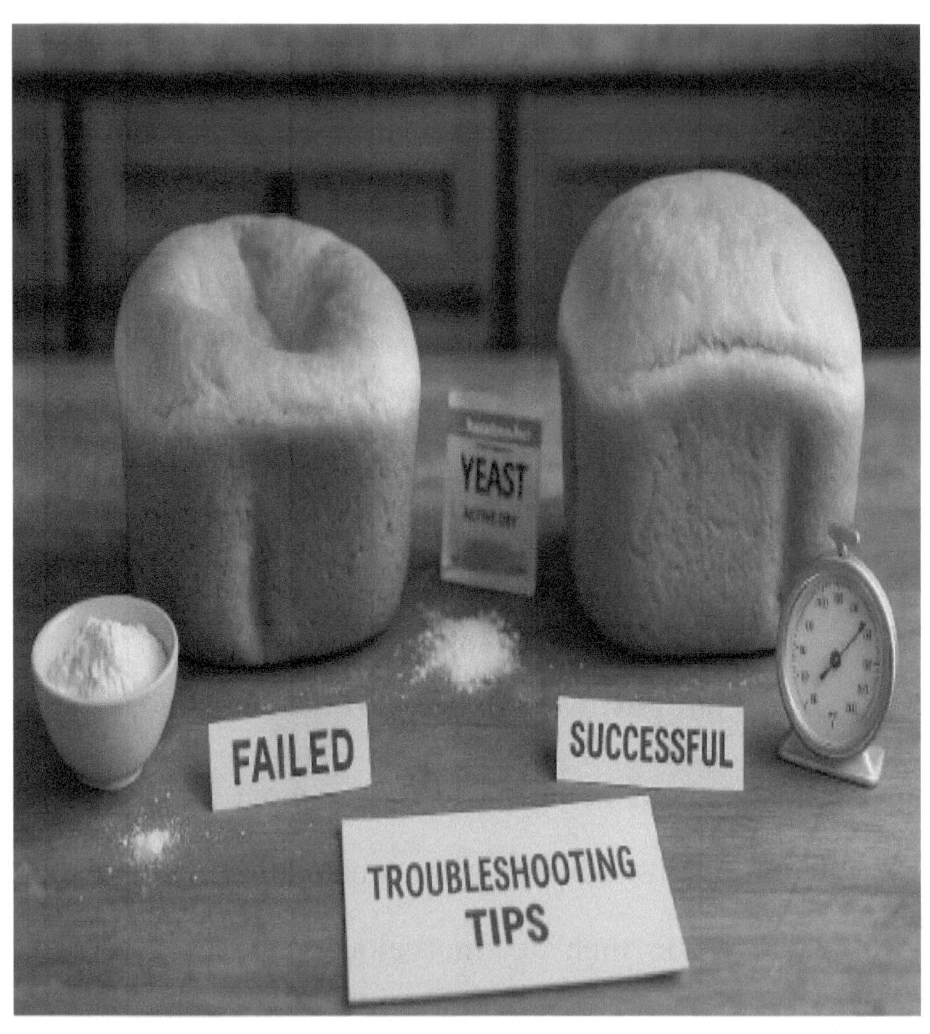

YEAST
FAILED
SUCCESSFUL
TROUBLESHOOTING
TIPS

Acknowledgments

To the quiet hum of my bread machine and the scent of warm loaves that filled my kitchen—I'm grateful for every imperfect batch that led to something better.

To the home bakers who inspired this project with their questions, flops, and triumphs—this book is for you.

And to my family, whose patience, taste-testing, and honest feedback brought every recipe to life—thank you for reminding me that the best things are shared fresh, warm, and made with love.